I0441595

If I Could Change My Race: Real Essays by Real People

Guensie Grecy

ISBN: 1535334436
ISBN-13: 978-153534433

DEDICATION

To those who have not been given a voice

ACKNOWLEDGMENTS

I would like to thank all of the writers who's essays are included. This book would not be what it is without your honest and unique perspective.

Love one another

PREFACE

I asked 20 strangers from different parts of the world to answer the following question in a 1,000+ word essay:

If you could choose your race or nationality, what would you choose?

This book is a collection of their responses.

On the surface, this book is about race, nationality, and culture. Beneath the surface, you will find many layers of conviction and debate highlighting truths and opinions. These essays cover psychology, sociology, and public perception. The writers pull you into their world, and at times dare you to walk in their shoes. These essays are about pride vs. shame, oppression vs. privilege; assimilation vs. cultural rejection; love vs. hate. More importantly, these essays are about people.

I want to make it clear that I don't necessarily agree with what is said in a lot of these essays. I became emotional reading some, for various reasons. However, I believe these voices are important. I chose to include these essays because they are honest reflections of the people who wrote them. I think it's important to listen to and have conversations with people you don't agree with, as it is a catalyst for learning and understanding others perspectives.

When I look back and try to think of how I came up with the idea for this book, I struggle to pinpoint an exact moment. I must admit, the racially charged events of the time brought race to the forefront of my inner dialogue. Battling waves of emotions, I wrestled with the feeling of helplessness. I asked God, what should I be doing? I believe He put it on my heart to use my gifts to foster a conversation. It was like a sudden epiphany. I'm going to ask people if they could change their race, would they? I immediately began working on it. I thought this would give insight into the way people view different races from a global perspective.

I assigned aliases to each author in order to protect their identity. I also decided to keep editing to a minimum in order to keep the authenticity of the writer's voice a priority.

Enjoy.

JANE

I'm 33 years old, white, and British.

If I could be any race and any nationality, I would be white and British.

My life has always been pretty easy. I was born to middle-class white parents, both university graduates, and went to university myself. I've always done well in life, without ever having to try too hard. For years I took all of that for granted and imagined that that was how everyone else went through life as well.

Then I married an Indonesian man, and everything changed.

I married this man because I love him. Like many couples, we met, fell in love, got married, and had two children. My parents, who had lived abroad for many years, didn't comment on the fact that I wasn't marrying a fellow Brit. My friends, many of whom were expatriates themselves, and married to foreign nationals, didn't comment on it either. I myself thought nothing of the fact that we are from different countries and of different races.

The first sign that things were not as equal as I had thought they were, happened shortly after we were married. Having gone on holiday, we were stopped at immigration and my husband was taken away and put in a little room somewhere in the bowels of the airport. I was allowed to go to baggage reclaim, free to do what I wanted. I was 3 months pregnant at the time.

My husband was handed a piece of blank paper and told to 'write down everything you know about your wife'. Perplexed at such a broad question he asked for an example. 'Write down her name and date of birth'. My husband did as he was told and released. At the immigration counter we had handed in our passports and the immigration officer had only seen our faces. These things alone were enough for him to suspect that our marriage was fake and that my husband had married me so that he could get a visa. A brown-skinned man and a white-skinned woman were obviously a red flag.

It didn't stop there.

After our daughter was born my husband entered our picture in an online competition about couples who had been in long distance relationships, as we had been for a while before we got married. In the picture, we are sitting in a park with our little girl between us; just like any normal family portrait. The picture was placed at the top of the website and got hundreds of hits and comments within a few hours. 'This picture is fake' was one of the main ones. Followed by 'I don't believe it' and 'Lucky him'. No one said that I was lucky. At the time I shrugged it off and we laughed about it, but now when I think about their reactions, I find it horrifying. To some people, it is more believable that models would fake a picture rather than the simple reality that a brown man and a white woman would choose to get married. The implication is that people with different skin colours don't mix.

Now I live in Indonesia, in a place with a pretty small expatriate population. When I walk down the street people shout 'bule' at me. It's an old word that originally meant 'albino'. Now it just means 'Westerner' and it's not used as a derogatory term as it once was. It doesn't bother me, but at the same time, it's quite clear that this is what I represent to the people here. I am a white person. Little kids often crowd around me, remarking on my looks. 'You have white hair and a pointy nose' they tell me, which anywhere else would be a good description of a witch.

Recently I tried to check into a hotel only for my credit card to be declined. 'It's fine just pay tomorrow' said the receptionist. When I asked if he wanted to take my I.D card as collateral he said it wouldn't be necessary. 'Well Westerners are more honest than Indonesians because they are more cultured' said my Indonesian friend, when I mentioned the incident to her. Apparently, the rationale was that white people, being of an elevated status, don't steal, tell lies, or commit crimes.

Even today, it's a common belief that I have seen myself firsthand. I have never been stopped by the police, questioned by immigration, frisked going into a nightclub, asked for my identity papers, interviewed about my marital status, or stopped and tested for drugs.

All of these things have happened to my husband.

On several occasions, he has been allowed to leave, or the questions have stopped when I have arrived on the scene. As if I somehow lend him legitimacy. He can't be that bad if he's married to a white girl.

I realize now that I have always been privileged, and if anything, the further away from the United Kingdom I am, the better I am treated. Showing a British passport at immigration almost anywhere in the world usually gets me instant access, often without the need for a visa, often without any questions asked. I can live and work in many countries far more easily than most other nationalities, especially compared to my husband. It's rare that I am treated with suspicion or with malice; quite the opposite in fact. My passport and my race seem to protect me as I walk through life, whereas my husband is hindered as a result of his.

We now have two children and at the moment they have dual nationality and two passports, one British, one Indonesian. Under Indonesian law, they will have to surrender one of these at the age of 18, as dual nationality is illegal. When I mention this to anyone, British, Indonesian, or any other nationality, the advice is always the same.

'Don't let them give up the British one. It will make their life so much easier.'

I always reply that when the time comes it will be my children's decision to make and that I will support them either way.

But in my heart, I know they're right.

LYDIA

For some time now, I've wanted to start jogging and it wasn't because I was a health nut or loved the sensation of my leg muscles on fire. The reason I've wanted to jog is because when you live a tiny town in Northern Colorado, your house can become equal parts your sanctuary and your prison. That being said, I haven't jogged. I don't even walk in my neighborhood alone because sometimes I still see trucks roar by as Confederate flags flap in the wind just above the beds of the vehicles. I see them and I am afraid.

I wish I could say that if I could choose a race to be, I would just want to be myself. I wish that I would want to keep my brown freckled skin, and thick curly hair. Alas, I am half black, all the while wishing that I was white. I'd being lying to you if I said that I had never considered this question. I probably consider it more than I should. In fact, I'll tell you a day in the life of the girl I wish I was.

I imagine waking up to a room similar to mine in many ways. I'd still be me at my core and I'm not the most organized twenty-something, after all. Still, I would wake up to my mildly messy room, scratching my head and stretching my limbs. Here's when things begin to shift. I would shrug on the same size jeans, but I'd slide them up with ease. My hips aren't too wide and my butt doesn't stick out. Clothes fit as advertised. Hallelujah.

I'd then head to the bathroom and switch on the light. My blonde or brunette hair is messy but flat. I run a brush through it only a handful of times, avoiding damaging heat tools that need to be set to preposterous temperatures like 400 degrees. After that, I pull out my makeup. It was cheap and only in about four colors, from Ivory to Medium. I've chosen Light. Once I get to my lips, I go right for a bright pink. My coworkers will compliment it because I, as a white woman, know that many bright and fun colors will look lovely on me.

Then I get in my car, which is still awful but that's okay. I'll go to a dealership and they'll see me, knowing instantly that I am trustworthy before they see my bleak credit score. The car I will be offered will most likely be one of nicer models that the Mexican young man with similar credit was turned down for. Sure, credit is important but certain catch twenty-twos seem to be cut through with my magic white privilege scissors as if they're nothing.

As I slow to a halt at a stoplight on Main Street, I notice that a middle-aged black woman has been pulled over. Her brake light seemed to be broken and I sigh. I'd only just been pulled over myself for the very same thing but the officer was kind enough to let me go with a warning. My blue eyes catch the sight of handcuffs being pulled off of the policeman's belt loop as he roughly grabs the woman and turns her around, locking the metal braces around her wrists. He shoves her in the back of his car and I avert my eyes. She must've done something illegal. That's the only reason anyone gets arrested, right? It's none of my business. The stoplight turns green.

I arrive at my office and pass Bobby, a coworker of mine who's just a year younger than me and is currently gloating about his raise. I commiserate with an older Puerto Rican woman and a young black woman who is my age. They half-heartedly agree but turn to each other with rolling eyes when I sit down at my cubicle. I don't get it. They make the same as me, right? The one in the wrong is the guy who's making the most, anyway. Besides, if they're making less for some reason, they're just not as good at their jobs.

On my lunch, I walk through Old Town and strangers either smile at me or ignore me altogether. On the other side of the street, a black teenage boy is being stared at in shock and fear. It's as if the strangers around him believe that he has no place among them. An older white woman tightens her grip on her daughter's hand and crosses the street as soon as she sees him. I don't see this. I only see the boy and even I wonder what he might be doing.

After work, I eat my dinner at home and continue reading a book where the main character looks just like me. Of course, they don't need to. I'm sure I could read a book about anyone of any race. I just don't. The book - which happens to be about to quirky white people falling in love - is lovely

11

and, even though I've read many books about many quirky white people falling in love, I believe this one to be unique and unconventional.

I log onto Facebook just before bed and see that my friend from high school has posted some Black Lives Matter articles. I roll my eyes and refrain from commenting with my reasoning on why all lives matter. Clearly, some people see racism when there is none. As I continue to scroll, I ignore names like Mike Brown and Trayvon Martin and reblog a recipe I'll never use.

Ignorance is bliss and privilege is not only currency, but a shield. I wish it was perfectly fine to simply be me, but the one thing that society wants me to be is the one thing I can never change. Instead, let me be a white woman who will never know this fear, anger, and pain. Let me laugh at racial stereotypes because they never had the power to hurt me emotionally or financially. Let the cops see that I am non-threatening because, despite statistics, I am seen as the hero of every story. Allow me to be ignorant, I beg you. Who wouldn't want that?

LISA

To me, nationality is nuanced. I've been raised in a land that was stolen from natives to be built on the backs of imported slave laborers, and sadly much of identity is based on appearance. At first glance, many think I'm East-African; I get Ethiopian or Eritrean a lot! However, despite my curly, kinky hair, eyes that slant when I laugh, and brown skin, I reflect a blend of nations. I was born in Washington, DC and raised in Prince George's County, Maryland. My dad is from South America; his mother was born in India. My mom is from Jamaica; her dad is Chinese, and her mom is Afro-Cuban – born and raised in Jamaica. If I could choose my nationality, I'd choose to be exactly the nationality that I am. I am a mixed-American, sometimes referred to by the checkbox as an "Other".

What does it mean to be an "other"? For me, it means people ask me if I was born in the United States, or if I migrated here. It means when I'm filling out an application, I check the box that indicates I'm an "other/two or more races". When that option isn't available, I'm truly at a loss for what to choose. They ask me if my hair is real, if my hair is mine, and can they touch it. This question comes from people of various nationalities. It means that depending on my outfit of the day, I am looked at and judged as if I am either an African or Middle Eastern woman. And sometimes, people of Middle-Eastern, Indian, or African descent don't consider me "enough of" to be included in their group. It means that when I have children, I will have to talk with them about the prejudices that exist for all of people of color. I know…first world problems.

But, being an "other" has so many sweet spots. It means that family, education, and work are important, defining factors of each individual's make-up. Respecting my parents and elders is a huge deal to me, and my family. That respect translates into the way that my family respects each part of our culture.

I got to grow up in something that so many don't get to experience. My first words were spoken with a slight Patois accent. My wrists were always covered in gold bangles from my grandmothers since I was a baby. I remember home cooked meals with herbs, fruit, and vegetables from the garden – at the kitchen table with the entire family almost every night. When phone conversations with friends got cut short, it was often because I was called for dinnertime with the family. I got Jamaican breakfast every Sunday before church. Plantain and saltfish with ackee, dumpling and banana left the house smelling like Jamaica, but it had my stomach feeling happy and full. I got "flittas" (pronounced "fritters") every Sunday after church from my grandmother on behalf of my grandfather. I got to learn Chinese phrases before I touched that part of the globe and physically connected with that part of my heritage. I got to take piano lessons. I got to learn the value of a hard-earned dollar. I was privileged…and mixed.

In elementary school, I knew I was different. I went to a small private school, where I often found myself caught in a space of "other" and not fitting in because I did not fully understand the cultures that my classmates represented. I didn't see many kids who were like me. Some of my classmates made fun of my name on the sly. It was hard to make friends, so elementary school was a time that I spent mostly to myself. I mean, at school lunch when everybody else has a cool pepperoni pizza Lunchable with the mini crunch bar, I wasn't always super excited to pull out my peanut-butter, jelly, and banana sandwich. Little did I know, my parents were protecting me from processed foods. They were nourishing me and teaching me habits of wellness and prosperity.

Not having other kids like me helped me to live up to the "100%" policy my mother enforced with conviction. She wasn't happy, and I wasn't satisfied with myself if I didn't earn all A's every time report card season came around. The same work ethic carried me through my first few jobs as a hostess, waitress, and office assistant. After undergrad, I became a public school teacher. After years of working in the public school system, I decided to use the same dedication and work ethic to propel my freelance writing career. (At the time of my writing this, I'm two months into freelancing! I LOVE it!! Cheers for me!)

Our house represented all these different cultures. Of course, I didn't realize that our house exhibited all the cultural ethnicities of my entire family when I was younger. But, by the time I made friends in high school, when they would come over, their comments would show up too. "Why do you have a bunch of Buddha statues and Jesus crosses in the living room?" "Why do we have to take off our shoes?" "What are your parents talking about?" (When they'd converse with their foreign accents.) "Why does each room in your house have a different (tropical) color?" "Your mom offered me curry goat…what is that?" My American friends have come to love and appreciate what it means to come to my family home. In some cases, my friends have adopted themselves into the family. Truth be told, we wouldn't have it any other way. I digress.

My multi-cultural background allowed me to experience different parts of the globe from the safety of my home. If we wanted a Caribbean fete, an Indian ritual or ceremony, or an American barbecue, we simply called on family and invited everyone over for food and drink and fellowship. Half a decade later, I'm witnessing a growth in demand for diversity and inclusion. If I could choose my nationality, I wouldn't change a thing; my background has helped mold me into the person I am today; and I'm happy with who I am.

SARA

Over the twenty-one years of my life, I have heard the saying: "I am who I choose to be" so many times, but I have never really thought about it and its meaning, or asked myself: are people really who they choose to be? The answer should be easy because it is either "yes" or "no". Yes, I am who I choose to be, and I choose to be kind, honest, loving and generous... No, I am not who I choose to be: it has been passed to me by my parents and my ancestors; I was born Arab and Algerian, it is in my DNA and nothing can ever change that. Apparently, the answer is not that simple. Asking questions is part of the human nature, no one can stop themselves from doing so, and I am certain that I am neither the first nor the last to question: what if I could choose my race and nationality? Who would I be?

I would be Arab; I would be Algerian.

People might say that my answer is biased (by my own self). Maybe it's because being Arab and Algerian is all I have ever known, but being proud of my legacy and ethnicity is an innate quality that I cannot simply change. At the same time, I have other reasons that can justify my choice.

First, the Arab and Algerian history is so great (yes, many races have a great history, I could choose to be European and Greek for example, but I also want to be part of the great future that I believe we will hopefully have soon). Many modern and foreign researchers acknowledge that Arabs were one of the very first nations to develop the fields of medicine, literature, mechanics, science and astronomy. Optimistically, our young generations will be able to prove themselves as worthy successors to the best predecessors. Algeria is the largest country in Africa and one of the richest. However, it was occupied by many monarchies, empires, and countries (Romans, Ottomans, Barbers and French), before it became the country we know today. In other words, the inhabitants of North Africa have been influenced by several civilizations over the centuries. As a result, modern Algeria has a long history and a big archive.

Second, our rich culture: there is not a nation that has not been affected by globalization; however, some more than others, and I really think that we, Algerians, are still keeping so much from our Arabian and Maghrebian culture. Our language: dialects might differ from one country to another; however, most Arabs are able to communicate together, but if one cannot understand a dialect, the other can simply speak in standard (classical) Arabic. Our mother tongue is one of the hardest languages to learn, and I was very lucky to grow up in Algeria learning it at school. It seems so easy now (many Algerians and Arabs who have grown up in foreign countries want to learn Arabic, but find that very difficult). Speaking of classical Arabic, which is one of the richest languages, I must refer to the Arabic literature, or what we call "el adab", which emerged in the 5th century but started a long time before that. Arabs wrote poetry, biographies, romance, prose, theatre and epic literature.

I cannot talk about culture without mentioning the Arabian food. Algerian food was certainly not made for diets and people who want to be fit, but its incredible spicy taste makes all the calories worth it, since our ancestors' major activity and surviving necessity was harvesting. We have many dishes like Kouscous (made from semolina) and different homemade breads that are the base of our cuisine.

Finally, most of Arab countries are Muslims, and luckily for me, I was raised in a Muslim country and among a Muslim family. My words may sound racist, but I am sure that other people with other beliefs are as proud as I am of their faith. I totally respect that. Actually, even my religion obliges me to respect other religions and never insult any kind of follower of any belief. As God says in his holy book: "Do not argue with the people of the scripture (Jews and Christians) except in the nicest possible manner - unless they transgress - and say, "We believe in what was revealed to us and in what was revealed to you, and our god and your god is one and the same; to Him we are submitters." [29:46]. Many people relate Muslims to Islamists; as a result, Islam's image has been destroyed nowadays. I believe that it is my duty to say that Islam is a religion of peace and no Muslim is allowed to kill any human being without a reason no matter what, Islamists are extremists who kill under the name of Islam, and I really hope that the whole world will soon understand that they are terrorist and not people who fight for our religion.

To conclude, one's DNA cannot be changed; though, we can be both who we were made and who we want to be. It does not really matter from where we came. What does matter is that we are all one kind: the human kind. We should treat each other as equal people, and understand that one cannot simply be better because of his colour, tongue, religion or race. Whether or not we are satisfied and proud of our ethnicity, we just have to know that it does not stop us from being our own selves and act as individuals with what we believe is best for us and for other people living around

ALEXANDER

The question is, if I could change my race, which one would it be? As a philosopher, I have to define clearly what the race is and stick with it. At school, I was taught that there are three races: Caucasian, which stands both for European people and Arab people, Negroid and Mongoloid. There are discussions about Native Americans, as they could represent the fourth race, but most of the scientists believe that people from Asia traveled to North America long ago and settled down there. However I would like to devote a few lines to Native Americans, so we'll consider them as a fourth race.

I was never really into a quiet and stable life, but that's exactly what I have with the life of a white human in Russia. It's obvious that white people dominate. Their culture is way more significant (not necessarily bigger) than culture of Asian people or African ones. Europe was the centre, the main power of our world for centuries. Furthermore, white humans had ensured a dominant role in the future politics, culture, anything else. They had been pressuring and subordinating other races and their history is bonded tightly with the history of European conquests. Being white, after all, is the most comfortable and successful turnaround for me.

In my dreams, I'd love to be Native American Indian. I was always really passionate about their culture, Aztecs or any North American tribe. You know, if I were Indian I could ride around the whole continent on my horse, shooting arrows and hunting. I sense an essence of freedom in this way of life. I could be deep in the jungle. I could pray to violent and mysterious gods, talk dead beautiful languages and live the life of the warrior. But those days are gone. Aztecs are no more. Their culture is gone. Indians are on reservations. Their horsemen are still riding looking for game, but it's not the same as before.

So in the today's world I would love to be black. It's quite an irrational choice, right? Black people have been humiliated for years. Today they still have to fight for their rights and place in society. Due to this, they had troubles developing their own culture and it, although it is significant, cannot be compared to culture of Europeans or Asian people. The next question obvious: what is so appealing to me in the black race?

First I have to explain what I value the most in this life. It's the sense of interest. At each phenomenon in the world I look from this perspective: is it interesting or not? All other values step back for a while. It is important if the thing is good or bad, beautiful or not, true or false – but that is in second place. So here is my first premise to my answer: I consider black people to be interesting.

Not just like that. There is nothing special about black guy in Africa. But the country where I live is the country of white people. In the context of being surrounded by whiteness, black people become interesting. What brought this black guy here? What's the story behind that black girl? They are special. In some ways it's tragic, as they were cut from their homeland, from their families. There is always a story behind them. It doesn't work this way with white men in black countries. There he is a tourist or conqueror or businessman but certainly, he is not there due to some beautiful reason. There is no dramaturgy in his presence there.

When you are white among whites there is no connection between you and people in the street, no friends, no enemies, you are all the same. When you're black in the country of white people, it's different. Complex and diverse relationships suddenly appear. Here is man looking at you with hate. He doesn't like you, and doesn't want you in his country – an enemy. Here is a woman who has never seen a black guy before. She looks at you in wonder. Here is a beautiful white girl, who at first glanced at you because you're different, but then smiled because she likes you – a possible ally. Then you see in the street another black guy you don't know. He doesn't know you either, but you look at each other. You nod. You may even shake hands – because he is your brother. He is from your tribe. He, for some strange reason, got stuck in this world of white people too. If you become friends, this may be the best friendship you've ever had – because you're opposing this unfamiliar, sometimes hostile world together. That's way more interesting than life of white humans among other whites.

I clearly understand that people are different and black people are different too. They can be violent, rude and evil and it seems like even more often than white people, due to a lack of cultural upbringing maybe. I'm not declaring this or trying to accuse anyone. Maybe that's the reason why Rastafari were not able to stand together as a united black clan. There were too many differences among them.

I still would like to claim that family is probably the main value of black people. We can take a look at soul food as a part of black culture to prove it. Contemporary American cuisine is actually a heritage from African slaves. Black people were servants in houses of whites and due to this were responsible for food. What were they cooking for themselves? For their table they were receiving what was left from master's meal. If master had pork and chicken, they would receive pork skin and legs, chicken wings, stuff like that. To this, they would adapt all the recipes and cooking techniques they were using in Africa. That's the way soul food appeared. So American cuisine is a blend of African cooking heritage and products that slaves had in the New World. This includes things like fried chicken, cornbread, and sweet potato pie. You name it. It is not all that respected in the world, as such food is heavy, junky, and not really healthy. But there was always one and very important characteristic of soul food: it is always for family. It is for the whole black nation. It's a food that brings family to the table, the food that you share. I think it's the key moment in black culture and way of life. You always want to have someone to rely on. To survive in a hostile world you have to stick with your brothers, with your family.

That's what I find really appealing about black people. The world of white humans is a world of grey people. They are all quite the same, more or less, good or bad. It looks boring to me. It's realistic, but in this perspective, you are content with being grey, you know that it's normal. But when you know that in the world there are people that are just like you and people who are different, with different cultural backgrounds, as it's the case for black people, you're devoted to your tribe, to your family. You don't betray it. You stay true.

MELANIE

I am a 24-year-old woman who lives in the United States, but both of my parents were born and raised in Guatemala. Whenever someone asks me what race I am, I find it hard to answer since I don't think I fit into any of the three main racial categories, but I identify myself as Hispanic. If I could choose my nationality, I think I would still choose to be Guatemalan because there are so many aspects of my culture that I love, but at the same time, I recognize that living in the United States also gives me certain privileges that I wouldn't have if I actually lived in the country I'm from.

My parents were lucky enough to enter the United States during the late 80's (albeit through a long and difficult journey). This was before the process for immigrants from Central and South America to become United States citizens was as arduous as it is today. When people think of Guatemala or any country in Central America, it's probably common to imagine certain things: poverty, gangs, people having a lot of children and living in poorly built houses. From the trips I've taken there myself and the stories my parents tell me, I know that, to a certain extent, these perceptions are true. Of course, there are people living well in that country, like everywhere, but there is undoubtedly a difference on the large-scale of the quality of life between Americans and Guatemalans.

Although I am proud of my country, I would never choose to live there. So while I would still choose to be Guatemalan, what is even more important to me is living in the United States. It's hard to say what my life would look like if my parents never left their country and they raised me there. I like to think I would have been able to go to college and find a decent paying career, but that is all just wishful thinking. Living in the United States, however, made going to college not only a possibility but a necessity.

My parents raised me and my siblings with the expectation that we would go to college right after high school, do well, and find a great paying job—a luxury they never experienced themselves. Now that I am an ESL teacher and am lucky enough to make a good living, I come into contact with immigrants on a daily basis. Most of my students are coming from El Salvador and Guatemala, with the hopes of doing the same thing that my parents wanted for me—going to school and making better lives for themselves.

Seeing the struggles of my students, many of whom have younger siblings they need to take care of and who work every day after school to contribute to their household, makes me think about how much it matters where someone is from and how that affects their economic success in life. Wouldn't these students have had an easier life if they were born in a different country? Or even further, wouldn't these students have an easier life if they were born white? Stereotypically, white students live in better neighborhoods—they attend better school districts and have more privileges than their black and Hispanic peers. Of course, this is a major generalization, but it's still an impression left in my mind and the minds of many others.

While I was searching for a teaching job, there were some districts many teachers simply wanted to avoid because these neighborhoods had a reputation for having troublesome students and fewer resources. These districts, without exception, were primarily in black and Hispanic neighborhoods. To the contrary, the most prestigious districts with the highest standardized test scores have a staggeringly large percentage of Caucasian students. Is there is a difference in the quality of education between these kinds of districts? If we go by measurements such as test scores, college admissions, participation in extracurricular activities, and so forth, then the numbers scream "yes!" We like to think of America as being the country where everyone can succeed, but how is that possible when children start off at such different levels?

Personally speaking, I attended a school with a large amount of Hispanic and black students. I think my success had largely to do with my upbringing and my own motivation to do well. Also, being Guatemalan probably helped me while applying to colleges. It's hard for me to say whether my nationality put me at an advantage over my Caucasian or Asian peers with similar grades and resumes, but it definitely did not hurt. In fact, it was a running joke at my high school about whether or not we should lie about our race—maybe check off that we were Native American—to better our chances of getting into a good college, and maybe even earning a scholarship.

When I think about why anyone would wish they were a different race, the only motivation that comes to mind is for economic or societal purposes. People have the notion that being white makes it easier to get a job; it makes it easier to make good money, which makes it easier to get a nice house in a good neighborhood, etc. On the other hand, people also have an idea of the struggles of being black in this country. It's harder to get and keep a job, more difficult to get yourself out of your particular neighborhood or economic station, and there's just more societal pressure overall. With everything that has been happening with the police and African Americans, race has never been a more sensitive subject. To a lesser degree, the experience of being Guatemalan or Hispanic—particularly if you are an immigrant—can be a difficult experience for many.

My light complexion and being born here gives me some sort of shield against the racism and negative stereotypes that I know many have gone through. I don't have an accent, but my mother does. My father has dark skin and an accent, and has recounted many instances of prejudice against him. I can see many advantages to being a different race, yet I would not choose to be something else; I also realize that this is because I have many privileges that people of my same nationality do not have. I am able to enjoy the aspects of my Guatemalan culture—the food, the holidays, the history, the land—all while enjoying my American culture..

PAUL

I am black. I'm from Nigeria, and I am 24 years old.

If I was given a choice on my race and nationality, I love being black; but the fact that we are discriminated against isn't up for debate. A few countries are known to be very unhealthy for a black person, and there are official shocking stats to back it up. So I guess I wouldn't choose another race (other than white) after picking a white country. It's not because I do not like my race. The goal of me being able to choose my race and nationality is to make a choice that would make me most comfortable and it makes no sense selecting Russia and being black in it. I'll be faced with tons of racial discrimination that would make me wish I was back to being black and from Nigeria.

For my Nationality, there are lots of picks, but I'll settle for any American. I would live in the state of Florida. Since I'll be a Floridian, I'll choose to be white. There are lots of reasons for my decision, and I'll run through a few below.

The average citizen (in Nigeria) is made to face countless hardships. I guess there are so many factors that come into play that makes it so.

There is a lack of social amenities. You'll be amazed at the standard of healthcare available to the average citizen. There are under-equipped hospitals, schools without buildings, etc.. These are the "Government" ones where the government subsidizes charges. Of course, there are better ones available, the ones by private entrepreneurs, but the charges are increased and made unavailable for the majority of the citizens. There are cases of people rushing dying relatives to the hospitals and being denied treatment for lack of money. In most cases the people end up dying for something money could fix. In the United States, at least health care facilities are available and made available for citizens.

I am a freelancer. Rates of unemployment are increasing. Well, unemployment is a world problem and not just unique to Nigeria. I require electricity and data to work. These are things remarkably inexpensive and free in most countries. As a freelancer, I have at times worked with teams of freelancers from other nations and was shocked at the price for data. A Canadian freelancing friend gets unlimited data for about $14 per month. A South African friend gets it even cheaper. Electricity is a terrible issue here too. A blackout, in most countries, is strange and is announced in the news. Here, if there isn't a blackout for 12 hours, it's an unusual experience, and we applaud our power suppliers. Not having power for two months or more is a regular happening. Everyone is left to provide his/her own power supply, which is extremely costly.

You might have noticed that Nigeria is almost always associated with scams. For that reason, the deeds of a few people have dubbed the national identity of a nation of more than 180,000,000 people. As a freelancer, when I am negotiating with a client, and he goes,

"You summed up what I need so well, I would love to work with you, can I know a little more about you?

I'll go ahead to say a little about myself, however, once I mention I'm from Nigeria, most clients disappear. A lot of them specifically ask for Americans to work on their projects. This distrust of Nigerians has led to most freelancers to adopt a foreign identity online.

I guess the PayPal issue can be added here too; a Nigerian PayPal account is basically useless, can't make transfers, cannot receive more than a miserable amount of money (about $200) and cannot make bank withdrawals. Guides to opening and operating a PayPal account are sold for about $100. You'll need tools to operate one, and in addition, your account is at risk of being "Limited" (PayPal's word for banned) anytime. All because PayPal assumes a whole country is full of scammers. Well, again, trust issues.

Communal wars, robbers, terrorists, terrorists and yet another group of terrorists. The security risks are many, and our security forces are largely unequipped to deal with them. I wouldn't say they're incompetent; they might be trying and know the reason they are incompetent to deal with this crisis and all. Of course, there are security risks in America and all over the world, but the attitude of the security forces at combating it plays a significant role in discouraging it.

As a citizen of the United States, specifically, (Florida), I wouldn't be subject to these difficulties; I'll get access to good social amenities, adequate security, steady electricity, affordable Wi-Fi, clients that' will want to work with me and freedom from being labeled a scammer.

My opinion is based on the fact that I am a freelancer and in no way reflects the entire populace of Nigeria. A political thinker might read this and say "What? You're concerned about free Wi-Fi? And you left 'this' and 'that' out." However, this is my take on the reasons I'll choose to be a Floridian rather than a Nigerian. Nigeria is developing and in some years would be great.

STEVEN

They say that you can be anything you want to be if you just put your heart to it, but no matter how hard I try I can't be a 6 foot 10 black guy who plays in the NBA. I'm still stuck here, in suburban New York, a 14-year-old Asian guy surrounded by rich white kids. Don't get me wrong, I love my town, my amazing high school with great teachers, and I love my community, but sometimes it feels like I'm like a little Kraft Singles slice of cheddar in a Swiss cheese fondue.

I don't hate all the rich, white, Roman Catholics that go to my school. I don't really hate anybody, but it pains me to hear stories of kids who are my age (slightly older maybe) smoking pot, drinking beers and having oral sex without any repercussions from literally anyone. It just sort of annoys me to see people throw their lives away just to be 'popular' and live out the rest of their lives on the trust fund that some old, dead, white guy who worked his ass off to give to his descendants.

If I were to be a race, other than my own, I would not want to be of the same breed as the people I mentioned before: the rich, white, materialistic, selfish and shallow kids. I would really only want to be born with that first adjective. If I were to live in the same place and retain my original personality, I would choose to be black. Now, why would you want to be a black guy in a white neighborhood? Well, I'd bet with my hard-working attitude, my intelligence, and no-nonsense demeanor, I'd be able to really make a change in the African-American and white American community and here's why.

My grade has one half-black guy (he's my best friend by the way) and he is one of the smartest, genuine and hard-working people in my grade. I had always known that people like him were underrepresented in media, since most of the black people you see on TV in our area, are basketball players and rappers. I had always wondered how it felt to break the stereotype. He always said that there were two ways to look at it; the positive way where he was just black enough to join an inner city pickup basketball game and white enough to go to the local country club without getting funny looks; or the negative way, where he wasn't black enough to prevent inner city thugs from calling him "light-skin", "half-blood" and "crackajack" and where he wasn't white enough to ask to go to a white girlfriend's family dinner. It shouldn't be like that.

I would make my friend's story and my friend's image the new stereotype, or at least far more commonplace than it is now. I would make the image of black people better and in doing so would prove to the American public that since not all black people (especially men) are gangsters, rappers or basketball players, then, not all white people are racist, bigoted, rich, gun-toting rednecks, and that not all Hispanic people are illegal, cheating, poor swindlers; and that not all Asian people are nerdy, weak slant-eyed chinks.

I would use affirmative action (which is usually quite unfortunate for me) and my already good test scores to get into a stellar university, fighting to change the image of black people there. I would then attain a government position, most likely governor, mayor or senator, and then fight hard to pass legislation for more law enforcement presence in the inner city, as well as tighter restrictions on crack and cocaine. I would then retire to a life of speaking at local schools, preferably poor, majority black schools and talk to them about making good decisions for a good life that can satisfy them better than crack or cocaine ever will. I would tell them to make good sex decisions, notably the use of contraceptive, good money decisions, in saving money and getting a job early, and good education decisions by telling them to finish the high school they are in now.

Now, what's the whole point in the last two paragraphs? Unifying the country by first getting the largest minority to be more included in the conversation by healing their image. This is how it would supposedly go.

First, let's start with the heightened law enforcement in the inner city. This is to stop crack and cocaine from circulating around and making the inner city a safer place for people and businesses.

Give it 10 years of intense law and order and the gangs will have left the streets, and young black men will not be turning to selling and using crack cocaine; and will instead have stable jobs in the businesses that have moved into the area due to the law upholding justice and making the area a safer place. With jobs to go to and things to look forward to, the number of single mothers will slowly decrease. The gang culture will dissolve; making the economic future extremely bright. Give it another 10 years after the success story of my state/city and the $20,000 median income gap between blacks and whites will be history and the country will be better united because of it.

All of this could be possible because in this fictional America I was a black man who other black men could agree and believe in. Only a strong, smart black legislator like me in my fictional world could unify the nation and put an end to the drugs, sex and gangster culture in the young African American community today.

I am someone who likes to get things done, and therefore, if I were to be another race, I would choose the race in which I could do the most good. I've talked to many black people about it and they mostly agree with my economics, but had a twinge of doubt that black people would actually listen to an Asian guy. This is why I would want to be a black man; so I could at least help to solve some of the problems that plague America; so that I could stop the police shootings and the racial tensions that come with it so we can get to other important issues that threaten America as a whole (ISIS, mental illness, mass shootings, climate change, etc.).

Which is not to say I don't like being Asian. I have a lot of pride in my heritage and my family's hard working 'immigrant morals', as opposed to the perverse morals of the rich white kids in my neighborhood.

DORIS

As human beings, we were born with the freedom of choice. This freedom to choose has spanned across all areas of our lives. We are free to choose what type of music we want to hear, what religion we want to be a part of, even whether we want to do right or wrong. Though sometimes external forces limit us from enjoying these freedoms, there are still some areas in our lives that we have no control over. We have absolutely no choice as to what our race or country of birth should be. However, being the dreamer that I am, I cannot help but wish that I could have a choice in these matters.

I am a 33-year-old single mother of a beautiful 13-year-old girl of African Descent. My daughter's skin is as dark as night. I was born in a South American country called Guyana, known as the land of many waters. I cannot overemphasize the fact that I love my country and my race with all my heart. However, I cannot help but wish that things might have been different. If I could choose my race and nationality, I would choose to be a White woman from the United States of America. This is because as a White American woman I would have more options and opportunities available to my child and me and we would be treated better.

Firstly, I must say that I choose to be white out of sheer frustration, desperation, and bewilderment. While I can live with the fact that it is hard to be a black woman, I simply cannot bear the idea of my child being discriminated against because of the colour of her skin and the texture of her hair. While I have learned to overlook being given a lower grade in college because my skin was darker than some bimbo head light skin gal, it aches me to my bones to see the dissatisfaction in my little girl's eyes every time she is being treated unfairly. Every time someone calls her ugly it tears my heart into a thousand pieces. She has sadly heard the word ugly so often that she has finally convinced herself that she really is. It is for these reasons that I wish with all my heart that I were white; then maybe here skin would not be so dark. Why should she feel that she was born cursed?

Additionally, I would choose to be white because my child would have more opportunities available to her. I am in no way advocating for a free pass for my child or myself. The last thing I want her to feel is a sense entitlement. However, there are certain areas where whites are given preference over blacks just because of the color of their skin and the texture of their hair. I want my child to have equal opportunity to compete with her white counterparts and have an equal opportunity to become the best that she can possibly be. However, this is a distant dream.

My final reason for wanting to be white is the safety that comes with belonging to that particular ethnic group. I am absolutely tired of living in constant worry that harm would come to my child because she is predisposed to be the target of ill will. Her chances of being pulled over by the police would have drastically reduced if she were white. I don't want my child to be part of a vulnerable group anymore. I want her to feel safe at all times. I want to feel at ease at all times, knowing that she will not be targeted because of her ethnicity.

Moreover, although I love my country and its people so much, I would still choose to be an American Citizen. The main reason is because the healthcare system in my country has left much to be desired. There are too many instances where persons are misdiagnosed, too many instances where persons lose their lives because of wrong treatment, and far too many cases of maternal deaths. I think the United States of America has a far more high-tech health care system, and I would most certainly be more at ease knowing that my child would be given the best care should something go wrong. I am tired of living in constant fear that her health needs will not be met.

Additionally, I would choose to be an American Citizen because there are far more educational opportunities available to its people. I believe with all my heart that education is necessary for positive transformation and my country is limited to one university that does even offer certain programs. For instance, if you want to become a lawyer in my country, you will be placed on a waiting list to go to some other country's university to finish off the program. This could take years since preference is given to the best in the class. There is little planning for special needs children, especially in rural areas. I have seen far too many young people get swallowed up in an education system that is not only uncivilized but also backwards. While I am not trying to disregard the fact that America has its fair share of issues, I still think that their education system is one that is envied by most developing countries.

Finally, I would choose to be an American citizen because there are more job opportunities there. I know that the unemployment level is still high there, but believe you me; it is far better than the situation in my country. The only promising jobs in my country are for teachers, nurses and police officers, who, by the way, are paid very poorly. The chances of young people earning a decent living are very thin in my country. Being an American citizen will greatly increase my chance of securing the means necessary for taking care of my offspring and me.

In closing, I wish to reiterate the fact that I really do love my race and my nationality. I appreciate the rich history and culture that being black is associated with. However, I am presently constrained by circumstances that do not permit me to become the best that I can be just because I was born to a different race and in a different country.

ANGELA

I am a 23-year old Black British female.

If I could choose my race/nationality... well, I would choose to be a Black British female. I have traveled to poverty-ridden villages and resided in cosmopolitan cities, seen first hand what it's like to be an Australian, American... to be Asian or Caucasian. Being Black and being British may not be perfect, but it's good enough for me.

I would choose to be Black and British because we are privileged. Yes, there is racism, crime, and a pretty lousy political system, but it is nowhere near as violent and cruel as other places in the world. Of course, I'm not blind to the fact that in Britain, some people are selfish and unwelcoming. There are those who use nasty words to describe immigrants, Asians, black people, white people, Americans, Africans and every other person that isn't British. However, being called the "N" word doesn't even come close to the phrases I've heard in reference to people of other races. It is no comparison to the life children in Laos have to live, nor Turkish children, nor Cambodian, and all the other countries that have areas with severe poverty.

I would be called every name under the sun if it meant children didn't have to drink dirty water or sell stolen goods just to have enough money to buy one meal.

I want to be British, because, I may not be able to do it alone, but I and every other British person have the education and facilities to contribute towards making a difference. Whether it is as small as being a pen pal to a boy from a small town in France to help him perfect his English, or volunteering in Ghana to provide fresh water everywhere. We can do it

I am from a city full of culture and colour. I'm from a place where I'm not afraid of starving. I'm not afraid of consistent racist remarks or people staring because I'm of a different race. I've walked the streets of Cambodia, where I felt completely out of place. I can walk the streets in Britain and not have hundreds of people staring right into my face.

When I was a child, I would have answered this question completely differently. I would have said I want to be an American, and I want to be Caucasian. Why? Because I wanted smooth hair that didn't turn into an Afro and that didn't tangle. I wanted to be pale because I didn't want to be associated with the slave trade and the mud beneath me. I wanted to be an American because they were portrayed to be so excitable, so fun, young, wild and free. As I grew up, all of my Caucasian friends wanted to tan and my views on being an American were tainted by the media with devastating crime and obesity. They ruined my American dream.

I now know that I didn't know then, that being black, just the same as being Caucasian or of any other race shows history and depth. I'm happy to be associated with the slave trade, to be questioned if my parents or grandparents were slaves. Neither were, but the conversation gives an opportunity for each person involved to learn. I know that the definition of an American isn't obesity and crime. I know these things because I am British, and being British has given me the opportunity to go to good schools, learn about the world, learn about the history of my ancestors, the history of my friend's ancestors, and even to understand that sometimes the media talks a whole lot of rubbish.

Right now, I live in Australia, where if you're black, why then you must be African. No? Well then you must be American? British? No way, it's not possible. In rural Australia, many, but not all people are naïve and uneducated. They haven't explored their own country let alone the world. I've met people who haven't left their small country town, people who don't own a passport, people who haven't opened a book about history, ever met a person of colour or a person who is bilingual. I'm not saying it's something to be ashamed of, but I do believe it's bad. How can you exist in a world you know nothing about?

I had a passport before I was 2 years old. I had been out of Europe by the time I was 3 and been across the ocean before I was 23. I truly believe that I've had these opportunities because being British is about uniting, learning and accepting. How could I do any of these things if I spent my whole life sheltered in my small town in London?

I straight away knew my answer to this question, but then I began to discuss with family and friends, which made me question what it would be like to a Hispanic girl, or an aboriginal from the tiny island of Torres strait. I'd love to experience other races and nationalities and embody them for a period of time but I couldn't choose to be something else.

How can I choose to change my nationality and race to a Chinese girl, who has been thrown on the streets just for being a girl, who in many countries can only get a job on a farm, as a kitchen hand or in a factory because my English isn't satisfactory?

How can I choose to change my nationality to a German girl, who is blessed with the opportunity to learn languages and study abroad?

British, Black... no, it's not the best, but when there are people like the Chinese girl who deserves better, and people like the German girl who have way more than needed, I choose to be me because I'm very, very lucky.

JERRY

Growing up, life was good. Being an African American male in Ann Arbor, Michigan didn't really affect me much. I always felt like I was just like all of the other kids and I never felt alienated or ostracized. Ann Arbor is said to be in a bubble of acceptance and open-mindedness. The people are well educated, and it proves that with education comes an understanding of other people.

With this being said, if I could choose to be one race, I would choose to be African-American. There have been times when I have felt like being White would make going through life easier, and I'm not going to lie, there have been times when I have wanted to be White. Being White in the world seems like an automatic advantage. Most places are accepting of White people and don't see them as threats. This isn't the same for Black people. Lots of places, including towns very near to my own, aren't accepting of my race. They tend to think of black people as a threat to their safety, and they treat them as such. I think this is because they have a lack of exposure to Black people. So, they believe whatever they see and read in the media. Being White definitely has its advantages.

I have just started my career in traveling and I plan to travel the entire globe. This might seem like an outlandish proposition. It is, but that won't stop me. I have read and heard that traveling as a Black person is risky business. However, I don't pay much attention to these warnings. I refuse to let other people's ignorance stand in the way of my viewing the world. I want to travel the world and show people that Black people are just like they are. We aren't threats to public safety or lazy or "ghetto". I want to expose people to a well-educated Black person that knows how to have fun safely. There will be places that I travel to that I'll be the first Black person that some of the locals have ever seen, and that thought excites me. Yes, I'll get stares, and yes people will be making assumptions about me, but that doesn't scare me.

In my opinion, African Americans are some of the strongest people in the world. We have fought our way from the literal bottom and now we're seeing ourselves reflected in high-ranking government positions. When I see Black people that are successful, I mentally congratulate them. No matter where you come from, there's no doubt that every single Black person will experience some type of negativity simply because of his or her skin color. African-American celebrities have fought their way through all of the backlash that not-so-open Americans spew at them on a daily basis. They show little Black girls and boys that they too can make it big in the world. Their options are not limited simply because they were born into a family that is categorized as African American. We are just as capable as any other race and it's time that we show this on a broader scale.

I would choose to be Black because I'm proud to be who I am. I'm proud to come from people that fought through so much hate and ignorance, only to prevail in the end. They didn't move to the back of the bus when told to. They didn't stop marching when they were spat on and attacked. They didn't stop demanding equal rights even when told that they were equal. As I grow up, I want to speak on this very topic. I want to show little Black girls and boys that their lives are just as precious as their classmates'. I'm so tired of people of color hating themselves and their skin colors simply because our media tries to convince us that light skin is prettier. Being Black is not a curse. It's a blessing.

I would choose to be Black because I wouldn't be who I am if I wasn't. Despite growing up in a very accepting town, there have been times while traveling or while watching TV that I felt inferior because of my race. This made me want to prove myself to the world. I didn't want to be another statistic. I wanted to excel in my own personal intelligence. I didn't care so much about grades or accolade. I just desperately wanted to constantly become smarter. I read a ton and spent more than enough time watching educational television programs. I would, and still do, get extremely offended when someone questioned my intelligence or didn't believe in my capabilities because I was Black. Whenever I found myself in these situations, I would only become encouraged to work harder. I am on a path of constant learning and I am very grateful to have the opportunities that I have. If I wasn't Black, I don't think I would have the love for learning that I have today. I don't think I would be as motivated to expand my horizons as I am. I simply wouldn't be me.

The last reason that I would choose to be Black is because I have an honest love for the positives of Black culture and history. I love reading about strong Black people of the past and learning about interesting traditions that Black people have. I think the Black culture is one of the most interesting because of the deeply rooted traditions that it possesses.

There are certain things that Black people in America have inherited from their enslaved ancestors. I think that there are certain things that we do that just simply run in our blood. I believe that Black people are magical and I wouldn't want to give up that magic for anything in the world. We are just as capable as anyone else on this Earth and its time that we all start to believe this. My life wouldn't be the same if I was anything other than what I am today and I'd like to thank the universe and God for making me just the way I am.

LAURA

Consider this. The average woman is born with 2 million eggs and typically releases one per menstrual cycle. Healthy men, on average, release 250 million sperm each time they ejaculate. Given the mind-boggling numbers involved, the likelihood of your existence is pretty low. What are the chances the precise conditions and perfect timing all combined in your favor?

When this thought first came to me, I mused out loud about the "improbability" of my having ever been born. Rather than sharing my sense of awe, a friend used that opportunity for a lesson in statistics, pointing out the probability of my existence was "1" because I had been born. Well, my ignorance of statistical terminology and the friend who was underwhelmed by my epiphany didn't dampen my enthusiasm at this personal revelation.

I have continued to mull over the idea that I have been incredibly blessed, so to speak. I use this term in the most secular of ways because I attribute my existence to pure chance rather than to any kind of supernatural design. On top of the dumb luck of simply being born, I was graced with starting life in a well-developed country, the United States of America. I was born into an upper-middle-class family. Finally, I was born with the right skin color, and we all know which one that is.

None of us is given the opportunity to select our race or nationality, at least not our nationality of birth; but if I were given the choice I'd keep the race and ditch the country.

It would be hard to openly admit that I prefer to be white in polite company. It's politically incorrect, of course, but how can I deny the obvious privilege my fair skin affords me, and the unearned benefits I've reaped from my Caucasian roots? After all, as a white American, I don't feel the heaviness of years of injustice inflicted on my people.

As a white American, I'm not directly burdened by the aftermath of slavery. I don't carry the weight of my ancestors' suffering, which has been passed down from generation to generation and continues to affect my community. I'm not slapped in the face and told by the majority that racism no longer exists when clear evidence to the contrary abounds in the form of income inequality, incarceration rates, and countless other measures.

As a white American, I'm not marginalized. You won't find my family and me living on a tiny parcel of land that my People were allotted by the majority many years after our lands had been stolen and our way of life torn apart.

Just as I had no choice in my race, I had no choice in where I was born. My nationality was designated by the coincidence of my birthplace and my parents' nationality. Many would consider me lucky to have been born in arguably the most powerful country in the world. I can't disagree. Certainly, I could have entered the world as the citizen of an impoverished nation, one with a disgraceful human rights record, or any other number of disadvantages.

Just because I judge my birth nation doesn't mean I don't appreciate the positive things it offers. After all, being an American citizen is another aspect of the advantage I was born into, an advantage I did nothing to earn. Some self-labeled patriotic types have a hard time accepting critiques of the United States and try to shut down detractors with a love-it-or-leave-it attitude.

This is exactly the closed-minded mentality I would love to escape. It is the reason, if I had been given an option from day one, I would have chosen to be Scandinavian. If I had to choose a nationality within the Scandinavian countries, feel free to pick the name out of a hat, draw straws, or toss a coin. Maybe Denmark. Perhaps I would choose Denmark because it's attached to the European mainland, which makes travel to other areas more convenient. Other than geography, the specific country wouldn't matter much to me. In general, the overall values and priorities of the Scandinavian countries reflect my own.

I prefer a secular society, where rules and norms are based on reason, where religious values hold no power over what I choose to do with my body, whom I choose to love, and what my children are taught in school.

I appreciate a society that values the family by providing for adequate vacation time, covering paid maternity and paternity leave, and ensuring its elderly are well cared for in their later years. I stand behind a society that uses its resources for the betterment of its people, such as offering debt-free quality education, rather than funneling a large portion of its budget to making devices intended for the destruction of others elsewhere in the world.

I believe in a cooperative society where I help you out when you're down and you agree to do the same for me. Here in the US, there seems to be a sense of scorn towards those who must rely on the social safety net, a safety net that is woefully inadequate, I might add. My friend, a fellow American who works in the helping profession, who has contributed to society since the day she became a working adult, recently found herself without work which also meant no access to the medication she needs to function on a daily basis. This is in spite of the so-called Affordable Care Act.

Reflecting on the benefits Scandinavian countries offer their citizens, I wonder why I haven't looked into ways I might leave the US to make a life for myself in what I consider a more suitable place that reflects my values. In the words of my ultra-nationalist compatriots, if I don't love the US, why don't I leave it? I suppose that in spite of its failings, the United States of America is still my home and that counts for something.

VANESSA

Immigrating to another country is hardly ever simple, especially for young children. As they grow up in a new environment, they also assimilate to its culture. This survival process can birth two conflicting personalities. At home, these children are taught to be the embodiment of their native culture, but the minute they walk out the door, they shape-shift into a personality that has been fine-tuned to its surroundings. Occasionally, these sometimes-contradictory identities can become fluid. One might find themselves acting "American" in their Indian home, or vice versa, acting more Indian with their American friends. The time will come, however, when immigrant children will choose what mask they want to permanently wear - the one of home and tradition, or the one that has been fine-tuned to their surroundings, or one that is a combination of both. However, no matter what they choose, they will find that their struggle has only just begun.

My parents and my brother immigrated from India to Chicago in 1992. I was born two years later, officially an American citizen at birth. Thus, growing up, my brother and I were absorbed in two cultures, Indian and American. At home, our parents made sure to instill within us the lifestyle, traditions, and realities of the Indian culture. To us, they were the representatives of a world that my brother and I would never experience. To them, we were not just carriers of Indian genes but also of the culture they had to leave behind. However, outside the walls of our home, beyond the reach of our strict parents, my brother and I had learned to adjust to American culture. We were both fully up-to-date with American lifestyle and traditions, in all its facets, from music to fashion, to its common beliefs such as self-independence.

It wasn't long until we learned that even though American culture was constantly changing, Indian culture was not. There was no "American way" that could alter the ancestral history book our parents ruled our home by. They made that rule clear with lectures and punishments for daring to challenge the status quo they strove to uphold. On the other hand, there were occasions where our Indian ways seeped into our lives outside of the home. I found that I was more reserved, conservative, and competitive in social situations. I held myself to stricter, more pious standards compared to my friends, such as refusing to date boys or placing a curfew upon myself despite not being given one. I found that I had stronger wills to be the best person in the room, morally and intellectually, even when among close friends. Growing up, teachings of home followed me wherever I went. They always seemed to dominate my personality in social spaces, just like how remnants of American values made me somewhat critical of the Indian-cultured person my parents were trying to craft at home.

There comes a time in every person's upbringing where they are finally ready to walk out the fitting room, identity proudly in hand. For immigrant children, the choice isn't always easy. For instance, I can choose to be solely Indian, a choice my parents would most likely approve of. On the other hand, I can also choose to be solely American, a more socially acceptable decision. Here's the rub. Would either choice be authentic? How can I pick one identity without acknowledging the influence of the other? I, and many others like me, have struggled for years to find a solution that would appease all parties, including ourselves. Unbeknownst to us, the answer to this complex crisis was simple – a hyphen. This punctuational correction allows us to present a more accurate picture of ourselves, an intersection of two defining identities, such as my Indian race, and my American nationality.

Nevertheless, choosing our identity is not the end to our battles but rather the start of another one - acceptance. Many do not understand that a difference between race and nationality could exist, especially in communities where one's race aligns with their nationality. This became apparent whenever I traveled to India. I was constantly teased over trivial things such as not knowing the regional language or being oblivious to common cultural traditions I didn't practice at home. The distance I felt between my relatives and me made the divide between nationality and race abundantly clear. The awareness of a gap returned many years later in college when two Indian friends who had recently migrated to America called me "white-washed" when I told them I didn't call my older brother "anna," a term used to show respect to elders. I realized then why I have and never will be accepted by other Indians, and why my brother will always be considered more Indian than I. To them, I was simply "too American" to even be called remotely Indian.

But what does "American" mean? The standard answer is that there is no true definition. America is a "Melting Pot" of cultures and people. However, if one picks up a history book, they will learn that the definition of "American" has often times been exclusive. Anti-immigrant and anti-minority sentiments have stained the inclusive values the United States of America represents.

However, it was the tragedy of September 11th, 2001 that sparked a new wave of racist mentality towards the Desi (brown) community. Anyone who appeared remotely Muslim was suddenly considered a terrorist. I was in the first grade at the time, living in a small town in suburban Cleveland. I was the only brown person, and person of color, in my entire grade. Therefore, I was the class representative of persons of color, especially after 9/11. One classmate even told me her mother didn't want me at her birthday party because of my color and Indian background. A few years later, I moved back to Chicago and into another predominately white town. My friends made it clear through constant micro aggressive remarks about my culture and color that I was Indian first instead of American just like them. To this day, I struggle to decide which was the greatest tragedy of 9/11, the loss of life or the idea that the differences between Desi and American cultures somehow makes us less American than everyone else.

There is an urban saying that perfectly describes the common predicament that first-generation immigrants face, "Stuck between a rock and a hard place." Immigration has given a unique chance to choose our identity, whether we wanted to be Indian or American or to celebrate their intersectionality by creating a hyphenated version of both. We quickly found that no matter what choice we made, we still had another fight on our hands, being accepted by either side. People who use differences as an excuse to create division instead of inclusion judge us. These are people who refuse to look past slight variations to see that despite our location or our background, we still have the same blood running through our veins and the same spirit swelling in our hearts. We faultless children are thus exiled to amid nowhere, too foreign to have a place to call our home.

JASMIN

If I was ever stopped in the middle of the street and asked if I could choose my own race, what would I be, I would immediately reply with my current race, black. It would be an easy answer. However, after spending some time carefully pondering that question, I began to interpret it as choosing whether to live like I've always lived, with my tradition and my culture or choosing a life of least resistance. I understand that there aren't only two races in the world but as I battled back and forth with myself about this question, choosing between being Caucasian or being black was what it came down to.

I am black, a 100% African girl with fully blooded Nigerian parents. In the 21 years I have been living on this earth I have had the privilege of living on three different continents. I am one of those 'too foreign for home, too foreign for here' types, which although it might not be so great at times, has allowed me to experience different cultures and hold opinions that are completely free from cultural bias.

To me, black is beautiful, but I don't mean beauty in the shallow simple sense. I only find things to be beautiful when I feel deeply and passionately about them. Being black is beautiful, the way maybe the moon might be beautiful, not because of how it appears on the surface but because of how it makes you feel just by it being in the sky and shining in all its glory. Being black means tradition. It means a rich history and a rich culture, especially as an African. I can go back to my father's village today and step into a completely different time period, with their simple mud huts, and wells, and minimal technology. It's great and it's something I wish everyone had a chance to experience. I myself cannot imagine not being able to experience that. Being black and African means being unique, in the way I dress, the way I speak and the way I see things. It is such a great way of being.

On the complete opposite side of the spectrum, I remember that often being black is associated with pain and suffering. I mean how many times have you seen a representation of poverty as a thin sickly black child with all the pain evident in the eyes of the black mother? How can we discuss suffering without bringing up the millions of black human beings being shipped off like logs to serve a country. They are expected to serve a country that would one day insist they leave and find a home which to them is non-existent, after stripping them of everything they are and being done with them.

Being black means walking into a store in the western world and being profiled as something negative and have the workers follow you around (I experienced this quite often as a kid). To me, it also means being reminded constantly as a woman that my skin color makes me somehow less beautiful or less desirable. I have really seen and heard of this too many times. I mean have you ever researched about what countries have the most beautiful women? I always laugh it off at first but eventually these little things begin to chip away at your sanity.

I can't lie and deny the fact that I have sat and thought deeply about how much easier my life would've been if I was white, granted they have been for what I see now as ridiculous reasons. Nevertheless, I have and I hate that. But if I am being completely honest with myself, then I admit life throughout history and today, life does seem a whole lot easier for white people. In my opinion being white has become synonymous with being preferred, everywhere on earth, and yes even in Africa where black people are the majority. Walk into anywhere as a white person in Africa and you will be admired and more or less have anything you want handed to you. I say Africa in general because I have lived in more than one African country. I have had white African friends and the contrast between the way I lived, the way I thought about my future and the worries I had were so significantly different than theirs. A lot of people would probably disagree, but I can only comment on what I have seen. Based on my experiences, I do believe white is preferred even in Africa.

Let's not forget all the countries that are a mixture of darker skinned and lighter skinned people. This includes countries such as Brazil , India or anywhere in the Arab world and Africa. Have you seen how much the skin bleaching companies make? I am a Black Muslim. Having lighter skin is somehow interpreted as being better. This shouldn't even be a concept and is only a flaw in our humanity. Yet it is still very real.

If humans were better than this then I would have no problems being black in any lifetime. But they aren't. So yes, after giving it some thought I have come to the conclusion that I would choose the easier life. I would choose the life where I don't have to worry so much about whether people will like me less just because of my skin color. I would choose to be white. This is not because I don't see myself as a particularly mentally tough person who can't handle that and being black requires so much strength, persistence, and perseverance. This could also just be a case of me perceiving the grass to be greener on the other side.

Just a few months ago I witnessed a rant from a girl who believed that society is moving towards a preference for black features, and shames you for not having them. I was honestly surprised anyone held that opinion. So, I don't know. What I do know is, in this life, I have been gifted with black skin and I am glad for everything that I am and everything I have experienced because of it.

HARI

There are times in my life when I tinker on the window sill on the faintest of nights and gaze into the star filled sky. The serene and tranquil nature of the darkest hours always gives me ample to think about. I guess that's the time my mind is at the peak of its thinking prowess.

These thoughts often bring about their own rejoices and chills. That's how life pans out. There are moments of joys with spine-tingling fears in between. But as the joyous marks sink into the oblivion and fade away, the scars of fear never heal and never will.

Born in the mid-90's in the South Asian nation of Nepal, often styled as the 'Land of Gautam Buddha' and the 'Land of Everest', I've had my moments of welts and scars. I've had moments that questioned the ubiquity of my existence.

Nepal, a pretty scenic nation, home to the great Himalayas and rivers, is a sight to devour. It has its unique culture and traditions leaned into with the finest of artistry. But as the world has the unequivocal rule of classifying people into race and nationality, Nepal hasn't been left behind.

With a race and caste system to inbound the diverse nature of people, we contemplated national unification. In fact, the ancient ruler of Nepal and the first conqueror of the unified Nepal, Prithvi Narayan Shah labeled the nation as the common garden of 4 races and 36 castes. Looking back, these words seem lost in the current culture of the nation.

The caste and race system isn't wrong on its own. It's when the judgmental views start leaning towards one race that the negative sliding occurs. As is the case with a garden where roses take all the plaudits, those that are the in-power supremos in Nepal have over shadowed the other races and castes. These are the times when I dwell upon the mystified nature of proclaimed unity with the race and nationality divergent.

Hailing from the country's subordinate suppressed race, I felt the climate of living through second-class treatment as a citizen. The designated race in power had the extremist approach to other races and ethnic groups. Often, the sentiment of "why wasn't I born to the in-power race?' resounds deep down inside me.

In 1996, a couple of years after I was born, civil war broke out. The rebellious armed conflict took place. Rebels had the agenda of overcoming the monarch and the discriminative caste or race system The war gauzed the nation for 10 years when the political fruition came together to dethrone the king and the monarchy. The nation became republican and secular . More than 15000 lives were sacrificed and a 100,000 more were internally displaced in the battle for supremacy. But did that put an end to all the turmoil? Nope.

It did grant the citizens some powers and rights with the sense of achievement. However, the ongoing political shifts have engrossed the nation in tight clutches. Having a stable government is the key to development in the nation, which we've hardly ever seen. The ongoing battle for the power chair has made a mockery out of the nation's reigning system.

The 10-year rebellious conflict had little undoing on my childish mind as I grew up in the capital suburbs of the nation. I guess I was too small to understand it at all. Growing up over the years and reading into the things that happened, I muster the reasons why the conflict occurred. The vague childish memory of the conflict within me is now burgeoned with the dire image of it. These definitely raise questions inside me over the stance on nationality.

It's usually during the serenity of the night when I end up with these crippling thoughts. I have my fair share of thoughts. I've harbored dreams of settling abroad. away from the national chaos and the racial favoritism of my homeland. Honestly, everyone's always on the lookout for the better opportunities.

I've been quite a sports maniac since childhood. The preferable sports for me were cricket and football. Every South Asian is pretty crazy about cricket, aren't they? I was just about the same, supporting New Zealand on the international front since I was a kid.

I followed just about every cricket move of New Zealand and joined in on the rugby scene as the time went by. Following sports closely, I garnered a soft spot for the nation as a whole. I had always read about the scenic beauty and the peaceful nature of New Zealand. I loved how they ranked in the top of the most non-corrupt nations in the world. With all of that, I was pretty sold on the idea of moving abroad when the time came.

Apart from that, the European and American nations remain a dream for many. They represent a dream getaway to the best of the world. They represent a dream fulfilled life. The sense of a meaningful life abroad certainly arouses the imagination in us. No one's really immune to these thoughts.

The thoughts don't always materialize and end up fading into the vicinity. As I stepped into my early 20's and skipped the nation for a place in another neighboring nation to pursue my higher education, my laid back stance changed quite a bit.

I don't hold a grudge against my nation or with my race. It's just that everyone wants to have the best of opportunities. I felt the same way as a kid. I wanted to enjoy the best of moments of my life. However, as my mind opened up to different avenues, I learned the tricks and trades of the world.

The world isn't as simple of a place as one envisions. The efforts to achieve the very best life is an ongoing battle. I guess I would fight the battle the same way I'm supposed to, without trading my race or nationality. No race or nationality is as easy as it seems. So I would live with my same race and nationality and look to better myself over time.

As for the thoughts of being born into another race or nationality, well that's for another life -if there's such thing as another life.

CARLA

I am a Brazilian girl. I'm 29 years old and I am Caucasian. If I could choose my race or nationality, what would I choose and why? I thought about all the countries I've ever visited and that I want to visit, the cultures that I've experienced and those that I want to experience. In the world, there are wonderful countries, each with its uniqueness, with its beauty and its culture.

First, I thought in Finland, land of Gothicism and melodic rock, and the Norse mythology is fantastic.

Then I thought I also like the Greek mythology, so why wasn't born in Greece? Besides having a wonderful culture, Greece is one of the most beautiful countries in the world. It has beautiful beaches and beautiful men. In Italy, there are also beautiful men and Italian cuisine is divine. There are also the stories of the Roman Gods. Another great aspect is the climate of Italy: autumn and its red tones, the diversity of colors in the spring, the summer heat, and winter snow.

But still, I could have been born in England, preferably in London, which is considered one of the most beautiful cities in the modern and controversial world. London, in itself, is more than a reason to be born in England. A place where it is impossible not fall in love and miss when you're away. London is magical and unique. It is a place where everything or almost everything is accepted. It is a place where you can be or try to be what you want and dream; a city that lets dreams come true.

What about the USA? The life in the USA is practical. All that you think of can be purchased online. The country has quality education. They live with more security in their quality of life. There are so many places to visit, such as, large ski resorts, national parks, and beautiful landscapes. There is a climate for everyone.

But if I'd been born in Cambodia, then I would have a healthier life. The people are warm and the country's culture is fantastic. The decision is a difficult one.

After much thinking, I decided that if I could choose the country in which I would be born I would choose to be born in Brazil. I was born in Brazil and choose to be born here again. Brazil, in spite of all the bad things that exist here, and there are many, is a happy country with a happy people. With all the difficulties we face in our daily lives, we manage to maintain a good mood, and always manage to solve our problems. We remain happy. We laugh at ourselves. We laugh at our problems, but when we need to make serious decisions, we do it. We are a working people, go-getters and optimists.

Here we also have an unparalleled cuisine, different foods in each region. Here there are feijoada, acarajé, barbecue, coxinha, brigadeiro, açaí and a variety of fruits that I can't get enough of. We could spend all day listing a number of delicious dishes we have in every corner of the five Brazilian regions. The food is made with a simple goal: to be tasty. In Brazil, we are privileged to have a huge variety of fruits that are always fresh and affordable. Here we find natural juices made to order in any restaurant. What about our landscapes? Brazil is rich in fauna and flora. We have memorable landscapes, blue sky, golden beaches and beautiful green forests. We have mountains, waterfalls, beaches, deserts and even snow from time to time. Here you can practice all sorts of sports from surfing to climbing. We have urban and modern towns and we also have historical cities from colonial times. The warm tropical climate prevails in most of the Brazil and this makes it enjoyable year round.

In Brazil, people are happy and affectionate. We're always singing and dancing, and showing affection in public is part of who we are. A hug, a kiss on the cheek, or a smile always makes someone's day happier. You'll never find people as receptive and sympathetic as Brazilians.

Our music is cheerful and contagious. The music is part of Brazilian culture and is a very important part of it. There are several unique styles. There's music to dance, to protest, to love, to rejoice and to thrill. There's music in the bars, beaches, and streets. There are songs that demonstrate the culture in every region of the country, from north to south. Carnival is an example of how music is important for us Brazilians. It's the biggest party in our country, where we dance and sing all the time. The Brazilian music scene is incredibly heterogeneous.

Brazilians aren't just black or white. They are also all shades in between. People in Brazil are descendants of Portuguese, Italians, African, Japanese, Lebanese and many others. The result is this unique blend of cultures and ethnicities. Brazilians are simply beautiful.

I know my country has many problems and difficulties. We still need to make progress in relation to health, education, and security. There is a lot of social inequality and corruption in politics. But even with all these problems, if I had to choose, I choose to be born in Brazil. We have a diverse and rich culture. We are a democracy and we are recognized by the foreign policy for being a peaceful country. Here we have freedom of speech. We have rights as citizens. We have no war and we have many natural riches. The Brazilian soul is beautiful, as beautiful as our country. As a Brazilian song says: I live in a tropical country, blessed by God and beautiful by nature!

CYNTHIA

With my country's stark contrasts, distinct culture and relaxed vibe, I am happy where I am. If given a choice in my next lifetime, I will still choose who I am and where I am now, a Filipino living in the Philippines.

I've traveled a lot and experienced a handful of cultures. The more I am exposed to what other nationalities have and do, the more I feel that I am best suited where I am. As a millennial, I am connected 24/7 to the big web. I know what's going on around the world at large. There is terrorism at the four corners of the globe and the Philippines is no exception. With everything that's happening in the Philippines right now, the political turmoil adds color to the country's serene backdrop.

A calm and bright afternoon beside the sea is accentuated by the loud parties starting at dusk. Take your pick of either lush mountains or white beaches, as these beauties are usually just a few hours drive. Take a dip into our deepest azure seas, perfect for diving or for adrenaline inducing water sports. The Philippines is far from being a paradise, but it's the contrast that makes this country exciting.

What makes the Philippines distinctive? There are lots of cities in Asia but nothing compares with my countrymen's' political highs and lows, triumphs and misfortunes as well as our achievements and notoriety. We may take the slow pace during the day but we are not calm. For most people my age, the day starts only at dusk. We Filipinos can be laid-back and relaxed but if challenged, we will aim to surprise. Our colonial past has made Filipinos open and tolerant to just about any culture. We are open to change, in fact, adapting is our way of life. Filipinos are among the world's most trusted caregivers and healthcare professionals. It is our warm nature that makes us caring and humane.

In terms of education, Filipinos are natural learners. We are not as strict as Eastern Asians when it comes to academics but our professionals are among the best in the world. Our government doesn't yet have many resources to give free quality education to all, but we highly value education despite our lack of resources. We are not as hard working as our Japanese counterpart. We find a way to make everything easy and simple.

Filipino people are warm and natural conversationalist. We go the extra mile to make foreigners feel at ease in the country. Ask a sidewalk vendor for directions and he will gladly coax you in English. Almost everybody in the country can understand and speak English. Even all the signs are in this universal language. Our culture is diverse. Being influenced by Spanish, Chinese, Japanese and the West, our culture is a colorful and familiar mix of everything that is usable and good. We love to sing, and most of us are natural singers. Even those who are not as vocally gifted can deliver a good performance because we just love to express ourselves.

Being the country of choice for offshore business process outsourcing, our communication skills are as polished as native English speakers. We can go side by side with any country in terms of our ability. Likewise, we are still humble enough to do the most menial work, because we value our reputation. We do take work seriously. We also celebrate a day well spent with a hefty meal and revelry. We are mostly religious and content people. We take pride on forming friendship and enduring camaraderie.

Living in the Philippines is relaxed and affordable. The cost of living is among the least in the world because it is still a developing economy. Make no mistakes, our young population makes our workforce robust and competitive. Shopping malls, green fields and places of worship is usually situated side by side, conveniently located in just one town. You will never go hungry as there are lots of dining choices. A Filipino takes pride in producing savory food, not too spicy but more for the rich palate. We are not so much into online shopping. We love to hunt. Our malls are pulsating with energy every day of the week, not because we love to shop, but because we love to walk around and mingle with the crowd.

The beaches are top notch, unlike no other. Because we are a group of islands, the sea is easily accessible God has blessed this corner of the globe with pristine white sands and the clearest water. Our land is not tame, as we have at least 18 active volcanoes ready to erupt at any moment. The wilderness is rich with unique flora and animals; even our oceans are home to the world's biggest sea beasts. The temperature is comfortably warm and tropical. The atmosphere is laid-back. Time can be slow during vacations. Our landscapes are picturesque, but it is only recently that we had started to conserve our habitat. All in all, the Philippines is the perfect living spot.

The Filipino people may not be as disciplined as say, the Japanese. We may not be as old-world sophisticated as say, Russia. But Filipinos are the most resilient people that I have seen. Situated at the ring of fire, the Philippines is one of the world's top contenders for countries with the most natural disasters. Such a dreary and disastrous outlook is a stark contrast to the Filipinos' natural sunny disposition. We may get burned with lava and brimstones and swept with super hurricanes and year-long monsoon but Filipinos maintain an attitude as placid and carefree as summer. I don't know where this inborn optimism came from. All I know is that this same sunny streak is embedded into my psyche. It is something that I am proud to have, but more than that, it is something that makes me who I am. My fellow countrymen have yet to see my country's full glory. We have been through too much pain and oppression in the past, so I think it will be the good days at last.

JASON

Like all of us, I wasn't born into any race. Society inevitably inducted me into the race cult, and I have been at the center of two races ever since. One-half of my parents is a complete Mongolian while the other, an Aryan. As I am a fusion, let's just call myself Argolian.

I come from a small hill station called Darjeeling, in India, most famously known as The Queen Of The Hills. Darjeeling is a work of art; a painter's brush, a poet's words. She is nestled high up in the Himalayas where her lush green gardens of tea and majestic white Kanchenjunga compliment her beauty. Her year-round cold weather is a major attraction as well. It used to be the summer retreat for the British in India. Of course, we also have eighteenth-century toy trains powered by steam engines; courtesy of the British.

In India, people with Mongoloid features and backgrounds are all bundled up in the northeastern part of the country. The rest of the country belongs to the Aryans (north, west, central & east) and the Dravidians (south). That's basically how my country is distributed. We, the North Easterners, are infamously referred to as Chinkies. Although I am a mix, the Mongoloid features in me are more dominant. Thus, I am a "Chinky" too. This title doesn't come with much respect or affection. People from mainland India treat us like foreigners in our own country. We are harassed, beaten up and even murdered on several instances. We are asked to "go back to China" because of the way we look and dress. So much for democracy and secularism, huh? I fail to fathom where so much hate for your own countrymen comes from. Do you also treat your fellow citizens with such hate and cruelty?

People from Darjeeling (primarily Nepali speaking Mongolians) are very simple and basic. We work. We earn. We eat. We drink. We party (and our parties never end without a brawl). We send our kids to good schools. We brainwash their barely existent brains with ideas and God and expect them to grow up, get a job and look after their old parents. We never encourage them to become entrepreneurs or inventors. Wow! Can a community be more enterprising than this? Let's leave that for your amusement.

At the same time, the Mongolians are very hard working (more so physically). Somehow, I don't know why they seem to have more active hands and legs than brains. Hollywood has had an immense influence on our lifestyles, so has Western Music (The Beatles, Pink Floyd, Jimi Hendrix, Bob Marley, Led Zeppelin, Iron Maiden, ACDC, Black Sabbath, and the likes). We are a fashion conscious race. We would rather dress well than eat well. The Mongolians are comparatively more open-minded. And the most important part, they are better at treating women.

The Aryans, on the other hand, are slightly different. They too want their kids to get a good education, and look after their old parents. They too brainwash their kids with ideas, God and religion, and so on and so forth. But they are a more conservative race. They are so conservative that they do not just disapprove of homosexuality, they criminalized it. Yup, in India you can go to prison for being Gay.

[WARNING ALL GAYS OUT THERE]; we will send you to prison if you come to our country!

Again, very importantly, Aryans are not that good at treating women. Theirs is a more chauvinistic society. All their resources and priorities go towards the sons. Daughters have to take the back seat. They are seen more as a liability. To my utter anguish, women themselves are chauvinists. They are their own enemies.

Now, on the contrary, the Aryans use their heads a lot more than their hands and legs. This is why Indians have advanced so much in the field of science and technology. Just look at Microsoft, Google and PepsiCo (to name a few). They are all headed by Indians. As per a certain report, 36% of Scientists at NASA are Indians.

Houston, we have a problem. The Indians are taking over!

So with all these permutations and combinations, am I content with my race? Am I happy being an Argolian?

Naaaah!!!

I think I would want to be a Caucasian. If you're a Caucasian yourself, do you think yours is the best race? You probably have your own story to tell.

So, let us look at some of the reasons why I fancy the Caucasians.

For one, they are happier among each other. They can also be brutally racists, but they do not hate each other the way we do. The White direct their hate towards other races such as the Negros, the Hispanics, or the Asians, rather than another White.

Also, they've a ways been a very progressive community. Look at all the inventions they have come up with: telephone, railways, automobiles, airplanes, computers, the internet, rockets, and the list goes on forever.

What have we given to the world? Nothing!Yes, nothing. Russell Peters once said, "We Indians are so cheap, that we created the number Zero".

Even the Mongolians are not famous for inventing anything as such, the only feather in the Mongolian cap, I suppose, is Japan; they at least came up with the Bullet Train.

Anyway, the other thing I really like about the Caucasians is that they work hard and party even harder. They make an effort to compliment themselves for the hard work they put in and just let go of everything and have fun. That's how one's life should be, right? Happy all the time. So why not put in the effort to keep yourself happy? The Caucasians seems to have done a better job at this. The World Happiness Index has rated countries like Denmark, Switzerland, Iceland, Norway, Finland, Canada, Sweden, etc. as the happiest nations in the world; these are all predominantly Caucasian nations. India is somewhere at the bottom of the table. It just gives an indication of how unhappy we are with ourselves.

The Caucasians are more open-minded and free. Anything goes with them. Their lives are a lot more free from ideals, religion and God. They are way more realistic. We, on the other hand, are shackled in the chains of our own prejudice and bigotry. Most of the countries that have legalized same-sex marriage are Caucasian nations. Try doing that in India. You'll have your Honeymoon in prison.

The Caucasians also seem to have a successful life doing just about anything they like. It could be sports, music, acting, writing, business, storytelling, circus and so many other things. Here in India, you can only do three things: study hard and get a job or become a cricketer and if that doesn't work out for you, join politics.

Bollywood? Naaah… it's not for people with class.

We can all agree that powerful, largely Caucasian, nations such as America and England are big bullies. Don't believe me? Ask Vietnam, Iraq, Afghanistan and Libya. However, in their own country, and for their own people, they have created a world of freedom, creativity and equality.

One more thing Caucasians have impressed me with, is their manners and etiquettes. This is what separates us humans from animals. Don't you think?

So this is why I feel that Caucasians makes a better race than us.

But, in the end of all these, is this ok? Should there be the idea of you versus me; they versus us? Do we have to have a divide? We are probably better off without these classifications. If I had a magic wand, I would cast an Abracadabra over this whole wide world and completely erase the idea of "race". Because racism, along with other evils such as; religion, ethnicity, castes (in India), does more harm than good. It only divides people. These are mankind's worst enemies. How do I know this? Well, I live in India, which is the most racist country in the world, and I have been at the receiving end of racism.

So, why can't we live together as one supreme-united-benevolent race? The Human Race!

DANIEL

The insecurities of being judged by a certain color and how we will be treated is prevalent.

I am a Japanese-Indonesian and if I could choose a race; I would probably be your average white male.

I've had a lot of racist encounters but the one that shook my entire existence happened in 1998. It was then the infamous 'Peristiwa 1998', which translates to the 1998 tragedy, took place in Indonesia. Whether this incident ever had an entry in the Indonesian history books, I do not know. However, the memory will always reside in me.

In 1998, politics in Indonesia were unstable. Violence and riots against the government took place. This affected the economic growth, which crippled fast. The government then could not handle the public outcry, and there was an immediate rise in unemployment. Due to the inflation of food prices, the tension was building up.

During the crisis, the president stated that the protests would not change anything. He simply flew out of the country for a political meeting in Egypt later that day. Outraged, the public replied with a series of attacks towards the Chinese-Indonesians, who were supposedly 'holding back the economy'. In the ensuing chaos, protesters began attacking shopping malls and police posts. Anything that looked Chinese was highly targeted. The streets are littered with burned cars. Shops were burning through the night. Countless Indonesian-Chinese women were raped and many resorted to suicide. It was a living hell.

I was 4 years old at the time. I barely understood how the things around me worked. One night, my family quickly packed our stuff and put it in the car. I was clueless but I remembered rummaging through the wardrobe frantically for my favorite toy. We left the residential complex with a local hired-driver.

I was told to put my head down in the car. My family was hiding under the seats of our car throughout the journey. My curiosity was at its peak. I saw the flickering of red and orange lights. I heard screaming and when I took a glimpse out the window, all I saw was horror.

In that split second, my mother pushed my head down again but the image is always in the back of my head. It was gruesome. Everything in sight was red because it was burning. I recall looking at a wooden cart on fire with a missing wheel. A motionless man rested quietly beside it. The buildings behind him were blazing and the sky…there was no sky. It was covered in a blanket of smoke.

In no time, my family and I were at the airport. It was insanely packed. People were screaming and pushing, and the airport security guards were trying their best to maintain the situation. My dad disappeared into the crowds and came back with two men. One of them was a local with a tanned skin who sweated profusely and breathed heavily. The other was a short man with a cheeky smile on his face. The short one welcomed my family, and in seconds we were escorted to the boarding room.

Everything seemed to be at peace the moment we stepped onto the plane. Time felt like it stopped ticking.

I woke up the next morning, already in a van rolling down the highway with my family. I have little recollection of what happened next. I knew we landed in Japan, crossed the Sumida River and stayed in a small apartment with my grandparents. My Chinese mom did not get along with them well. Eventually, my Japanese dad decided to bring us out of Japan again. This was not the first time I moved out of Japan. I concluded that bitterness would always exist between the Chinese and Japanese due to past conflicts.

There were a lot of complications regarding our residency then. My family migrated to Singapore within a few months. Later we moved again to Vancouver, Canada. It took about four years to return to Singapore again. We stayed there for a long time before moving to Sydney, Australia, where I would find my true home.

Having to live in Australia for a lengthy time made me want to be white. It was great. I never encountered any racist comments and I could integrate into their culture well. I do enjoy the company of my white friends in Sydney.

There were no riots or any violence against my races. However, my white friends do get extra privileges outside of Australia. For some reason, whenever I went traveling to South East Asian countries with my white friends, I felt as if they had a better treatment. It could be the way the media portrayed the Whites as favorable over Asians. According to popular media, they are stronger, smarter and richer.

Although I am not emotionally charged about the events that have been happening, it seems to me that racism and discrimination will always exist. Although I always question my national identity, I wish that I were not color-coded.

DEREK

The I am a 30-year-old white male who has lived his whole life in Texas, and, given the choice, I wouldn't change anything about my situation. I know there's nothing revolutionary about this. Anyone reading this might think, "So the white guy wants to keep his privileged lifestyle – big surprise." I absolutely recognize my privilege, and I imagine anyone else who could recognize it would want the same. I mean, who wouldn't want this genetic trifecta golden ticket?

Being born in the United States is a privilege. I have experienced what I would consider financial troubles, but even in my lowest economic circumstances, I was still richer than the vast majority of the people on this planet. My biggest worries have been things like making car or student loan payments or bringing up my credit so I can buy a house' never where my next meal will come from or whether or not my family can find clean water to drink. I can vote on and criticize my political leaders without fearing for my life. In fact, a basic privilege I never even think about is the fact that I can simply step out my front door and not fear for my life.

Being born a male is a privilege. I was an extremely smart student in school, but I knew girls who were just as smart or smarter who didn't get as good grades as me. I've never been labeled ditsy or slutty or bitchy. In my professional life, I find my opinions sought out and heeded, where my female peers are ignored or even reprimanded. I haven't witnessed firsthand the wage gap between men and women, but I wouldn't be surprised if I benefited from that as well. During my time waiting tables, I kind of thought the women I worked with were at an advantage as far as getting better tips from the male patrons, but the truth is their tips were no better, and they had to experience all manner of harassment to get what they could. Meanwhile, I got by with mediocre sales and was even promoted, and was never criticized for my failings. I could certainly chalk some of it up to my genuine attempts to be a nice person to everyone and foster positive relationships with my superiors, but just because I am a good person doesn't mean I can't also utilize my natural shield of being a man.

Being born white is a privilege. I was always told that I could be and do whatever I want, and there was never anyone or anything in society that tried to convince me otherwise. I can't remember when race first became an issue in my conscience, but I do know that having grown up in a rural West Texas environment where everyone was the same color as I led to me not knowing how to handle myself around those who looked different. I was never rude or cruel to people of color whom I encountered, but I was always cautious.

My first friendship with a black person was in high school, simply because he was the first black person with whom I ever had extended exposure. I was raised to be tolerant of those who were different than me, but I did not have any opportunities to exercise such tolerance. But it was something that didn't affect me, so I didn't have to worry about it. I didn't have to worry about being bullied for my skin color. I didn't have to worry about not getting a job because of my skin color, although I sometimes thought that affirmative action was holding me down whenever things didn't go my way. Really I was just frustrated that I couldn't achieve what I wanted by my own merit. I didn't have to worry about how I conducted myself around white strangers to appear less threatening. And I didn't have to worry whenever I got pulled over by police – not once during a traffic stop did it ever cross my mind, that I was going to be arrested or killed. During my teaching years, while living here in Dallas, I would explain to my students that in situations like that, if you have done nothing wrong you have no need to fear. I could say this because I was never part of a "dangerous" demographic, so it was true for me.

Being born a white American male is an enormous privilege. I considered myself a beacon of wisdom as a teacher. I had more world experience by this time, so I thought I had it all figured out. I acknowledged that there was still racism in society, but I assured my students that my coworkers wouldn't behave that way. I got annoyed with students when they tried to play the "Race Card", not thinking that having been dealt such a crappy hand, it might have been one of the only options they knew of. Like many people, I heard "Black Lives Matter" to mean "Only Black Lives Matter", so I thought "All Lives Matter" was a clever retort. I never stopped to think that the implied message was "Black Lives Matter Also", that they weren't so stupid as to say everyone else sucks, but that this particular group was getting the raw end of the deal and needed some attention. I saw the protestors' actions as irritating, but forgot that protesting has to be so in order to be heard.

Then five police officers were killed in my city. All white men. And while this gives me pause, I would still rather be white than anything else right now. Because I am scared enough and struggling enough as it is with my privilege, I cannot imagine what others outside of my bubble must be going through. But I want to understand. I took my children to the memorial service for these officers, and I exchanged pleasantries with black attendees who couldn't get enough of how cute my kids were. Instead of pretending to be busy at a red light the other day when a homeless man approached my car, I had a conversation with him about the tragedies happening in our country. I made a connection, which was something he wanted even more than money. It's true I wouldn't willingly trade lives with that person, but that doesn't mean I can't empathize with him and treat him like a human being.